P9-CEN-974

EVERYTHING SUPER BOWL

SUPER BOWL SURPRISES

BY ERIC BRAUN

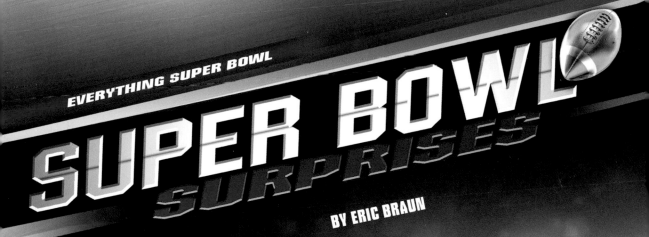

CAPSTONE PRESS
a capstone imprint

Sports Illustrated Kids Everything Super Bowl is published by Capstone Press
1710 Roe Crest Drive, North Mankato, Minnesota 56003.
www.mycapstone.com

Library of Congress Cataloging-in-Publication Data is available on the Library of
Congress website.

ISBN: 978-1-5157-2634-0 (library binding)
ISBN: 978-1-5157-2638-8 (eBook PDF)

Editorial Credits
Nick Healy, editor; Ted Williams, designer; Eric Gohl, media researcher;
Gene Bentdahl, production specialist

Photo Credits
Getty Images: Focus on Sport, 8, 12, 24; Newscom: Icon SMI, 25; Sports Illustrated:
Al Tielemans, cover (top left & top right), 7, Bill Frakes, 4–5, 20, Bob Rosato, cover
(bottom), 6, Damian Strohmeyer, 29, Heinz Kluetmeier, 21, John Biever, 26, John
Iacono, 18, 22, 23, Peter Read Miller, 10, 11, Robert Beck, 16, Walter Iooss Jr., 14, 15
Design Elements: Shutterstock

Printed in the United States of America.
009677F16

TABLE OF CONTENTS

SUPER BOWL SURPRISES

Maybe you've heard the saying "That's why they play the game." Maybe you've heard it a hundred times. It might be a tired line, but there's a reason it gets repeated so often. The team with the biggest names—or the team that looks unbeatable—doesn't always win.

That team might have huge stars and the best coach. It might have inspiring leaders and a fairy tale storyline that seems destined to end up just right. That team might be 18–0 like the 2007 Patriots, who had the greatest offense in National Football League (NFL) history. That team might seem like a sure thing.

But statistics don't win the Super Bowl. History doesn't win the Super Bowl. The Super Bowl often doesn't play out the way people expect. Weird things happen. Amazing things happen. Unheralded players perform like stars, and underdogs pull off upsets. That's what makes the game so fun to watch.

The Super Bowl ranks among the world's most beloved sports events, and its history is filled with surprises. That's why they play the game—because any player can come up big and either team might come out on top.

Collected in this book are perhaps the greatest upsets and biggest surprises in Super Bowl history. And, of course, the best stories are the ones that surprise us.

REVENGE OF THE CAST-OFF COACH

Jon Gruden loved coaching in Oakland. In four years, he had turned the Raiders from a last-place team into a serious Super Bowl contender. He did not want to leave—at least not until he'd won a championship there.

But in February 2002, Raiders owner Al Davis traded Gruden to the Tampa Bay Buccaneers for draft picks plus $8 million. Surely Davis never expected his Raiders to be facing Gruden in the Super Bowl eleven months later. But that's exactly what happened.

Tampa Bay had the NFL's top defense that year by a wide margin. The Raiders had a high-octane offense led by quarterback Rich Gannon. Unfortunately for Oakland, Gannon was still running Gruden's offense.

◄ John Gruden

To prepare his team, Gruden ran a practice where he played quarterback. He used Gannon's snap counts, Gannon's mannerisms, and Gannon's hand signals. He mimicked Gannon's pump fakes. When game time came around, the defense knew exactly what to expect.

Oakland scored the game's first points. After that, it was all Bucs. Tampa Bay's defense intercepted Gannon five times, and the Buccaneers rolled to a 48-21 victory. **"It was the greatest game I ever coached in,"** Gruden later said.

— WHOSE OFFENSE IS IT, ANYWAY? —

This wasn't discussed as much (probably because the Buccaneers won the game), but Gruden was running the same offense in Tampa as he had in Oakland. That means the Raiders knew *his* playbook too, but that knowledge didn't help them.

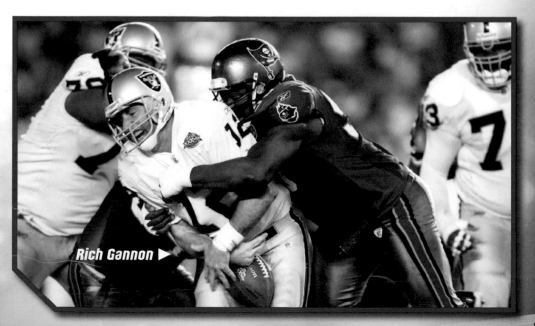

Rich Gannon ▶

PURPLE POWER OUTAGE

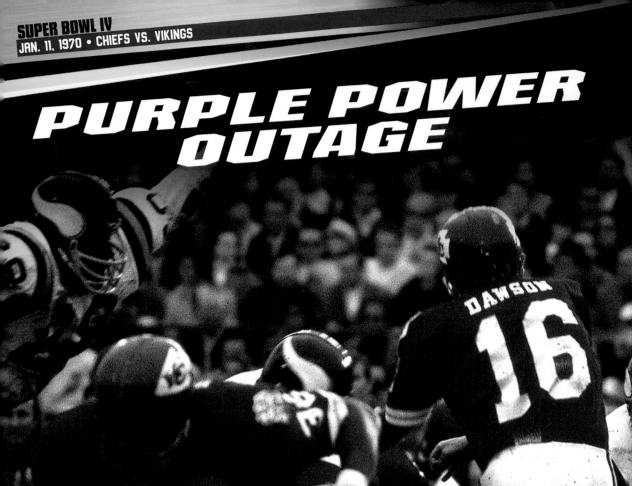

Most people believed the Minnesota Vikings would win Super Bowl IV easily. They'd gone 12–2 in the regular season. They'd scored the most points in the NFL and given up the fewest. Their defense was led by a fearsome line nicknamed the "Purple People Eaters." Their opponents, the Kansas City Chiefs, had gotten walloped by the Green Bay Packers in Super Bowl I.

In those days, the NFL and the American Football League (AFL) were still separate organizations. One reason the Vikings were favored was because they were in the older, more respected league—the NFL. But older wasn't necessarily better. Kansas City head coach Hank Stram later said, "Our styles were different only because the NFL had stood still for so long and resisted new approaches and ideas."

Indeed, the Chiefs offense confused the Vikings with multiple formations and shifts. They put men in motion in ways that NFL teams of that era rarely did. Kansas City scored on four of its first five possessions. Tricky reverses and a quick passing game kept the Purple People Eaters from getting to quarterback Len Dawson. The Vikings never recovered. The Chiefs won 23-7.

"I don't know if we were thoroughly prepared offensively or defensively," Vikings offensive coordinator Jerry Burns later admitted.

SAINTS SET AN AMBUSH

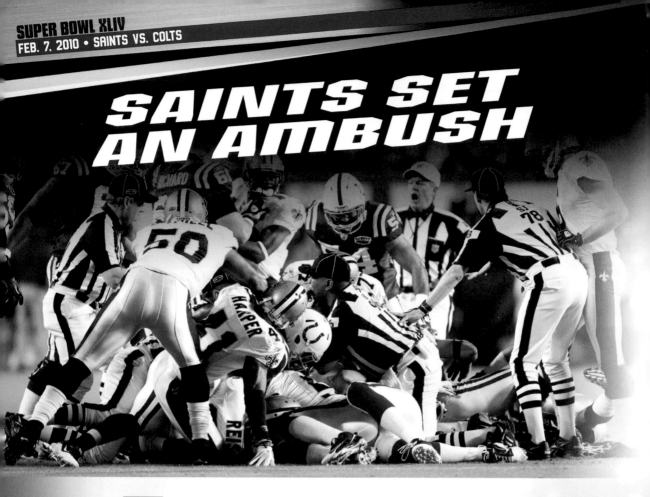

Team of destiny. That's what New Orleans cornerback Tracy Porter called the Super Bowl champion New Orleans Saints. As in, they were supposed to win it all.

Four years earlier, Hurricane Katrina had flooded the city of New Orleans. Nearly 2,000 people had died, and many others had been hurt or lost their homes. Sports didn't seem to matter at a time like this. Yet people needed something to celebrate.

— SHELTER FROM THE STORM —

The Saints' home stadium, the Louisiana Superdome, stands on high ground, so it became a storm shelter during the flood caused by Hurricane Katrina. About 16,000 people who had fled their homes ended up staying there. The dome provided a dry place, but it was hardly a comfortable setting. The power went out, and the water quit running. People there endured misery while waiting for help to arrive.

As the city began to rebuild itself, so too did its football team. The 2009 Saints flooded the scoreboard with points. When they met the explosive Indianapolis Colts in the Super Bowl, the game promised to provide plenty of offense. But at halftime Indianapolis led by a surprisingly low score of 10-6.

Tracy Porter ▶

Saints coach Sean Payton took destiny into his own hands. He ordered his team to begin the second half with a play they called "ambush." With the Colts awaiting the ball, the Saints kicker dashed ahead as if winding up for a big kick. Instead he dribbled an onside kick to his left. The ball deflected off a Colts player before Saints safety Chris Reis pounced on it.

The Colts were taken by surprise, and the Saints began a touchdown drive.

Late in the fourth quarter, the Colts were driving for a tie. Porter intercepted a pass from quarterback Peyton Manning and sprinted 74 yards for a touchdown. That was the end of the scoring. The Saints won 31-17.

Team of destiny? Maybe. But one thing was for sure: A city desperate for something to feel good about got just what it needed.

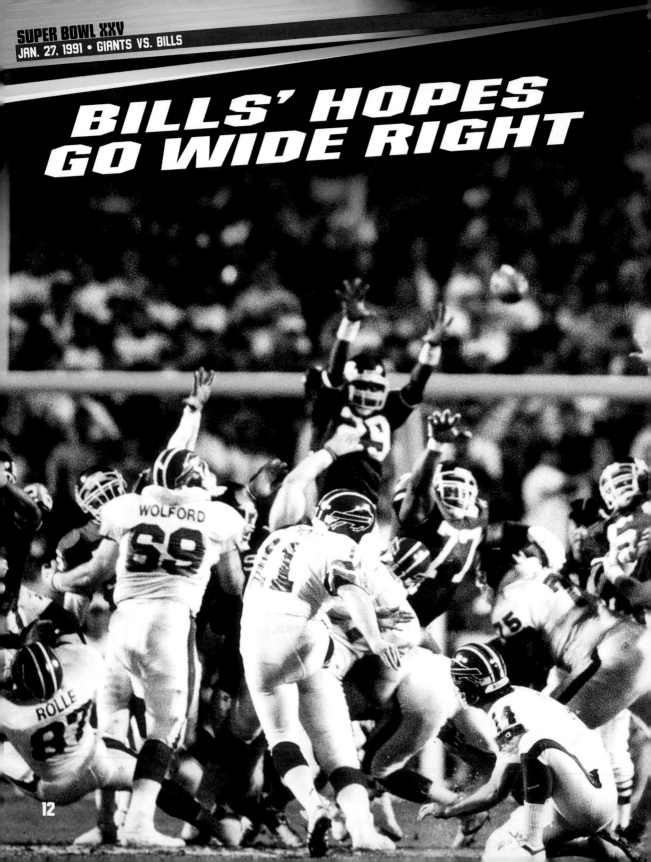

BILLS' HOPES GO WIDE RIGHT

The 1990 Buffalo Bills ran a fast-paced no-huddle offense piloted by quarterback Jim Kelly. They were loaded with superstars. Ten players from their team made the Pro Bowl that year.

Their Super Bowl opponents, the New York Giants, had recently lost their star quarterback, Phil Simms, to a broken foot. Their dynamic running back, Rodney Hampton, was out with a broken leg. Even their starting kicker was out with an injury. Everyone believed that the Giants were cooked. The Bills had more talent—and better health.

But the Giants were able to control the clock with long, bruising drives. They held the ball twice as long as the Bills. With the clock winding down in the fourth quarter, the Bills were down 20-19. All they had to do was get in field goal position for their reliable kicker, Scott Norwood.

Starting from his own 10-yard line, Kelly got them close enough to try a 47-yarder. With eight seconds on the clock, Norwood jogged onto the field. The snap was perfect. The hold was perfect. The kick was strong. It had enough distance.

Sportscaster Al Michaels made the call that to this day haunts Bills fans: ***"No good . . . wide right!"***

The super-talented Bills returned to the Super Bowl each of the next three years. But they lost each time. The one-point loss to the Giants was the closest they ever came to victory.

WILD CHAMPS

When the Oakland Raiders faced the Philadelphia Eagles during the regular season, things did not go well for Jim Plunkett, the Raiders' quarterback. The vaunted Eagles defense sacked the 32-year-old a whopping eight times on their way to the win.

Plunkett and the Raiders recovered from that ugly November loss. They finished second in their division and sneaked into the playoffs as a wild card team. The Raiders had a long, hard road ahead of them. No wild card had ever won the Super Bowl.

Although they were the underdog in all three of their playoff matchups, the Raiders kept winning. They were pumped up and ready for a rematch with the Eagles—this time in the Super Bowl.

The Eagles had just defeated the Dallas Cowboys in an emotional National Football Conference (NFC) Championship game. Over the past 12 years, Philadelphia had gone 2–21 against Dallas. Beating the Cowboys had been a major goal for the Eagles. Some Philadelphia players felt like that game was their Super Bowl. And some observers thought the Eagles were drained after their big win.

They had one more game to play. The real Super Bowl. The Eagles were favored, but they came out flat. If they expected to harass Plunkett the way they had earlier, they got a rude surprise. The Raiders mixed up their protection and kept their quarterback upright all game. Plunkett completed 13 of 21 passes for 261 yards and three touchdowns. He was named the Super Bowl's Most Valuable Player (MVP) after the Raiders' 27-10 victory.

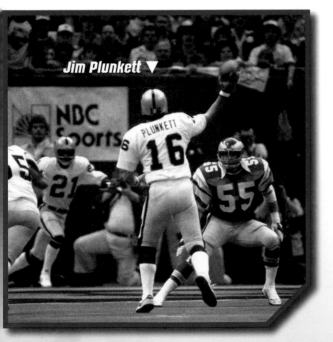
Jim Plunkett ▼

— WILD CARD WINNERS —

While the Raiders were the first wild card team to win the Super Bowl, five other wild card teams have matched the feat.

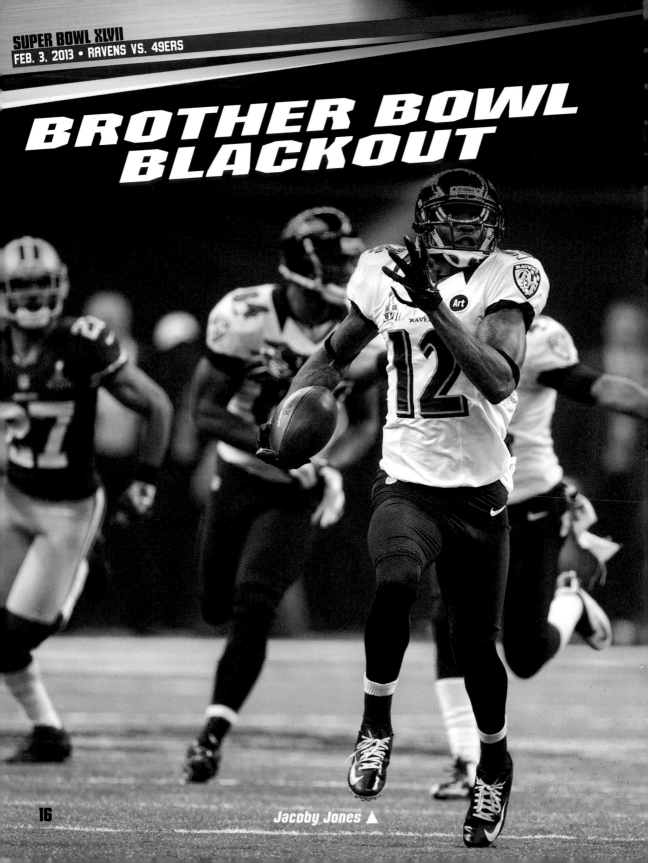

BROTHER BOWL BLACKOUT

Jacoby Jones ▲

Baltimore Ravens quarterback Joe Flacco tossed three touchdowns in the first half of Super Bowl XLVII. The Ravens' Jacoby Jones opened the second half by returning the kickoff 108 yards for a touchdown. The Ravens led 28-6 over the San Francisco 49ers.

Before the game, most of the attention had been focused on the coaches. That's because the two head coaches in the game were brothers: John Harbaugh of the Ravens and Jim Harbaugh of the 49ers. Much was made about the "Brother Bowl," and even their mom was interviewed. She joked that she wished the game could end in a tie. Of course there are no ties in the Super Bowl.

After Jones' TD return, it looked like a Ravens victory was in the bag. But then something weird happened: The lights went out. For 34 minutes, the players stood chatting on the field while the stadium staff tried to fix the power failure. It had to be the strangest surprise in the history of the Super Bowl.

When the lights flickered on again, it seemed to flip a switch in Jim Harbaugh's 49ers too. Michael Crabtree grabbed a 31-yard touchdown pass from quarterback Colin Kaepernick. A couple minutes later, Frank Gore ran six yards for another TD. Then the 49ers recovered a fumble and tacked on a field goal. Suddenly it was a five-point game. The blackout had led to a shootout.

In the end San Francisco came up short, and the two brothers met at midfield for a handshake. John Harbaugh later said it was a hard moment to share with his brother, who had just lost a heartbreaker. ***"A lot tougher than I thought it was going to be,"*** he said.

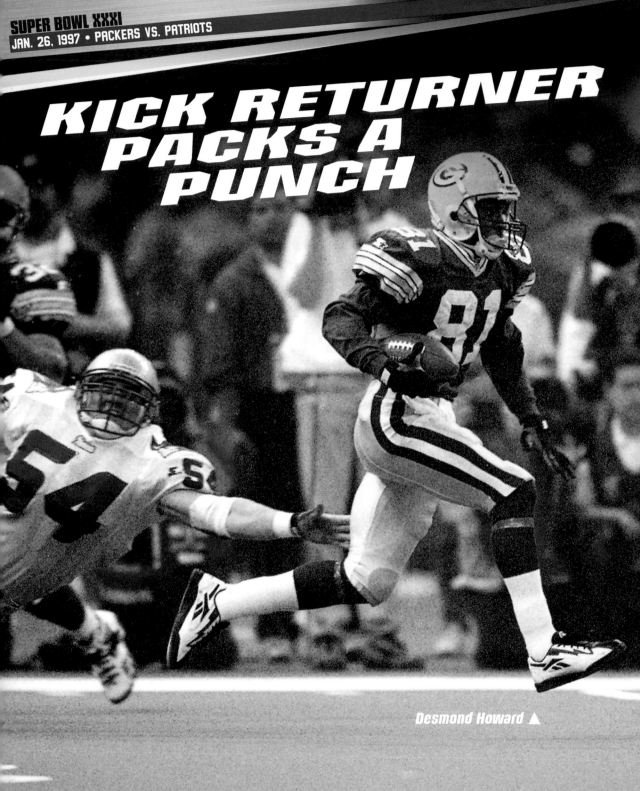

KICK RETURNER PACKS A PUNCH

Desmond Howard ▲

Here's a story about returns: Back in the early days of the NFL, the Green Bay Packers enjoyed an extended run as the greatest team in the game. Those glory days were long gone by the 1990s, though. The Packers had been a miserable franchise for more than two decades. Led by star quarterback Brett Favre and a fearsome defense, the team began a return to greatness. The 1996 team led the league in points scored.

Packers kick returner Desmond Howard was making a return of his own. In college Howard had been a star receiver at the University of Michigan. He'd won the Heisman Trophy. But as a pro he had struggled. It looked like his career might be over before the Packers signed him.

Howard made his presence felt early in the Super Bowl. On the Patriots' first two punts, he made returns of 32 and 34 yards.

"They continued to roll the dice by kicking it to me," Howard later said.

After a third-quarter New England touchdown, the Pats were down by six and seemed to have the momentum. They had a decision to make: Should they concede field position by kicking off short or squibbing it? Or should they risk kicking deep to Howard?

They chose the latter, and Howard cruised 99 yards for a touchdown. Though it was not even the fourth quarter yet, the game was essentially over. Howard ended with 244 return yards and was named MVP of the game. He had returned to the NFL in a big way. And he had returned the Green Bay Packers to the top.

A SURPRISING SHOW

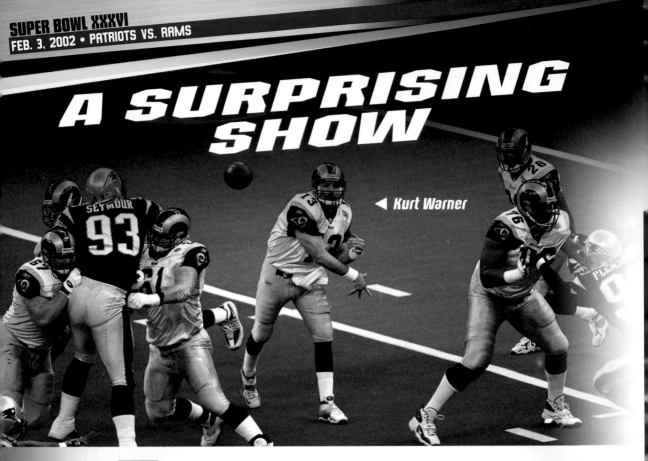

◀ Kurt Warner

The St. Louis Rams were heavy favorites in Super Bowl XXXVI for good reason. They had the highest-scoring offense in NFL history. They were built for speed and played their home games on artificial turf in their domed stadium. They had won the Super Bowl just two years earlier. Led by two-time MVP quarterback Kurt Warner, the Rams were known as "The Greatest Show on Turf." They also had a tough defense. It ranked third in the league.

Here's what most people expected to happen: The Rams would easily win their second championship. The game would establish them as a rising dynasty. The New England Patriots would lose big and sink back into their usual losing ways.

But the Patriots had one thing the Rams did not: A young quarterback named Tom Brady. At the outset of the season, most fans had never heard of Brady. He was behind the veteran Drew Bledsoe on the depth chart. But when Bledsoe got hurt early in the season, Brady took over.

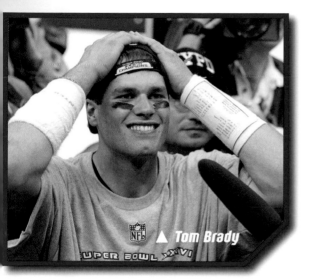

▲ Tom Brady

In the Super Bowl, the Patriots and Rams played a surprisingly close and low scoring game. The Pats had a lead in the fourth quarter, but the Rams scored to pull even at 17 with 1:30 left in the game. After the kickoff, Brady led his offense onto the field to begin a drive at their own 17-yard line.

In this spot, most coaches might opt for caution—let the clock tick down and go to overtime. But the Patriots' defense was exhausted. Pats' coach Bill Belichick knew if the Rams got the ball again, they would likely win. He told Brady to forget playing it safe.

With veteran-like nerves, Brady moved the offense quickly and efficiently, setting up the game-winning field goal by Adam Vinatieri. The 48-yard kick was no gimme, but Vinatieri drilled it. As it turned out, there was a dynasty being created that day. It just wasn't the one that most people expected.

— PATRIOT POWER —

With Belichick as coach and Brady as quarterback, the Patriots played in six Super Bowls from 2002 to 2015. They won four of them.

ELWAY WINS, AT LAST

▼ John Elway

There are great quarterbacks, and there are champions.

By the mid-1990s, John Elway of the Denver Broncos was surely a great quarterback. He was among the all-time leaders for number of touchdowns thrown. His arm was so strong, the ball whistled after he released it. And he had been to three Super Bowls.

Problem was, his Broncos had been totally demolished in all three.

— ELWAY VS. MONTANA —

John Elway lost his first two Super Bowl games by crushing margins. He lost his third in even worse fashion when the 49ers, behind quarterback Joe Montana, smashed Elway's Broncos, 55-10. Along with Dan Marino of the Miami Dolphins, Montana and Elway were the superstar quarterbacks of the era. Until Elway's final two championship seasons, his legacy had paled in comparison to Montana and his four Super Bowl titles.

Elway was 37 years old and thinking about retirement when his Broncos reached the Super Bowl again after the 1997 season. They faced the Green Bay Packers, who had won the previous Super Bowl and were easily the best team in the NFC. The Broncos seemed headed for another defeat.

Instead, Denver forced three turnovers, scored 31 points, and won an emotional victory for their quarterback, their franchise, and their city.

Broncos running back Terrell Davis ran for three touchdowns, but the highlight most people remember was Elway's "helicopter play." Imagine this: It was third and six late in the third quarter with the game tied. Denver had the ball on the Packers'

◄ **Terrell Davis**

12-yard line. Elway ran right and leaped toward the first down marker. Three Packers hit him at once. His body spun like helicopter blades, but when he landed, he had the first down. The old man jumped to his feet and pumped his fist. Two plays later, Davis barged into the end zone to put the Broncos ahead to stay.

As it turned out, Elway did not retire that summer. He returned for another season—and won another Super Bowl.

BROADWAY JOE'S GUARANTEE

With a nickname like "Broadway Joe," you gotta be good. And New York Jets quarterback Joe Namath was very good.

In 1969 the charming Namath was the face of the AFL, which had not yet merged with the NFL. Everyone believed the NFL was vastly superior to the AFL. It was the older, more established league. It had legendary franchises, including the Green Bay Packers, who had won the first two Super Bowls in blowout fashion. The AFL was like a pesky little brother: annoying and certainly not a real threat.

The Jets hoped to put an end to that notion. In Super Bowl III, they faced the Baltimore Colts. The Colts were another one of those famous NFL teams. Their defense was like a brick wall, having shut out four opponents that year.

▲ Joe Namath

Yet Broadway Joe promised the world that his Jets would win. When a Colts fan bragged to him that Baltimore would crush the Jets, Namath responded, "We're going to win Sunday. I guarantee it."

Namath used quick passes to negate the fearsome Baltimore blitz. Running back Matt Snell ate up yards on the ground. The Jets got up 16-0 and held on to win by a score of 16-7. Broadway Joe had lived up to his guarantee, and the AFL had won its first Super Bowl.

An AFL team defeated an NFL team again the next year, meaning the first four Super Bowl games were split, two apiece. The AFL had earned respect—largely thanks to Joe Namath and the Jets.

THE MERGER

In 1964 Joe Namath was drafted by the Jets and by the St. Louis Cardinals of the NFL. Namath chose the Jets partly because they offered him $427,000 over three years, a record at the time. The AFL had sudden appeal to players and began to gain popularity with fans. Soon the NFL reached out to the AFL to discuss a merger, which finally took effect before the 1970 season.

A GIANT UPSET

By 2007 the Patriots had established themselves among the greatest football dynasties of all time. They'd won three of the last six Super Bowls. Yet they wanted to get even better. The team went out and found more talent to surround Tom Brady.

In a draft-day trade, the Pats landed Randy Moss, who had been considered the greatest wide receiver in the game before a pair of quiet years with the Raiders. The team hoped Moss would return to form. They knew an elite receiver would help Brady and his teammates dominate on offense.

▲ Tom Brady

— PERFECT SEASON —

The 1972 Miami Dolphins went 14–0 during the regular season and won two playoff games to get to the Super Bowl. They beat Washington 14-7 in Super Bowl VII to complete the perfect season.

And dominate they did. With the infusion of offensive talent, the Pats of 2007 scored more points than any team in history. Moss caught 23 touchdown passes that season, a new record. Brady threw 50 touchdown passes, also a record. The Patriots destroyed the league and finished the regular season undefeated.

No team other than the 1972 Dolphins had gone undefeated through the regular season, playoffs, and Super Bowl. The Patriots looked like a very good bet to repeat the task.

However, one of the Pats' toughest battles to stay unbeaten had been against the New York Giants. In the last game of the regular season, the Pats escaped with a 38-35 win.

The Giants may have lost that game, but it was an important confidence booster. When those two teams met in the Super Bowl a few weeks later, the Giants players and coaches believed they could win.

DEFENSIVE BATTLE

New York's ferocious defensive line, anchored by Michael Strahan, pressured Brady all game with just a four-man rush. Through three quarters, the greatest offense in history had mustered only seven points. The Patriots held a slim 7-3 lead.

Early in the fourth quarter, Giants quarterback Eli Manning drove his team downfield and fired a touchdown pass to backup receiver David Tyree.

On the next drive, Brady found his stride. He took to the air, spreading the ball between three receivers and hitting Moss for the go-ahead TD with 2:42 left on the game clock.

Down by four points, the Giants needed a touchdown.

THE HELMET CATCH

The Giants quickly moved the ball. They converted a desperate fourth and two to keep the drive alive. Then they were third and five near midfield with only 1:15 left on the clock.

Manning dropped back and somehow broke free of two defenders who had him in their clutches. He floated a wobbling pass toward the middle of the field. Giants receiver Tyree was there, but so was the Patriots' Pro Bowl safety Rodney Harrison.

Tyree leaped and grabbed the ball, but Harrison got a hand on it too. Tyree began to fall back with the ball barely held in his right hand. To secure it, he pinned it against his helmet as Harrison fought to jar it loose. The two crashed to the turf. Somehow Tyree held on.

Completion. First down.

"Harrison made as good a play as he could have made," Patriots coach Bill Belichick said.

After the incredible helmet catch, the Giants cashed in with a touchdown and the win. The Patriots finished the season with the most sickening feeling that an 18–1 team could possibly feel.

David Tyree ▶

29

GLOSSARY

ambush—a surprise attack

blitz—a play in which several defending players charge toward the quarterback to tackle him

contender—a team that has a good chance to win a championship

destiny—what happens to a person or team, especially when it seems to be determined in advance

dynasty—a team that is successful for a long time and wins multiple championships

formation—the position of football players before a snap

legacy—qualities and actions that one is remembered for; something that is passed on to future generations

onside kick—a kickoff that is deliberately kicked a short distance so the kicking team can try to recover the ball and gain possession

squib—to kick a football on a kickoff so that it bounces along the ground

unheralded—coming without notice or fanfare in advance

wild card—a team that advances to the playoffs without winning its division

READ MORE

Braun, Eric. *Super Bowl Records.* Everything Super Bowl. North Mankato, Minn.: Capstone Press, 2017.

Editors of Sports Illustrated. *Sports Illustrated Super Bowl Gold: 50 Years of the Big Game.* New York: Sports Illustrated Books, an imprint of Time Inc. Books, 2015.

Hetrick, Hans. *Six Degrees of Peyton Manning: Connecting Football Stars.* Six Degrees of Sports. North Mankato, Minn.: Capstone Press, 2015.

INTERNET SITES

FactHound offers a safe, fun way to find Internet sites related to this book. All of the sites have been researched by our staff.

Here's all you do:

Visit www.facthound.com

Type in this code: 9781515726340

Check out projects, games and lots more at
www.capstonekids.com

INDEX